In Pensive Musing

Sarah Podwys

BookLeaf Publishing

Presentation by *BookLeaf Publishing*

Web: www.bookleafpub.com

E-mail: info@bookleafpub.com

ISBN: 9789357212366

First edition 2023

DEDICATION

To all the teachers that taught me how to read and write, but most especially Mama Squires (may she rest in peace). She taught me not to be afraid to write about anything.

ACKNOWLEDGEMENT

I'd like to acknowledge everyone who has supported me in my writing talent, reading and giving feedback of my work. My husband, Ivan Podwys, has been so very helpful when I write, whether it be poetry or anything else. He talks me through writers' block, helps me with research if I need him to, and is usually the first to read my work. Thank you to my parents, John and Dixie Sampson, for encouraging my developing talent as I grew up. My mom especially would read my poetry when I was living at home and it encouraged me to keep writing. They even paid to take me to a very expensive poetry convention when I was 18. I learned a lot there. Thank you to the English teachers I've had throughout the years. In particular, Mrs. Anderson, who took time out of her lessons to read my poetry to the class, despite poetry not being part of the curriculum in middle school special education. I'd like to also thank my friend Lily, who went through a lot of my poems with me a while back and suggested a few good edits. She also did some editing for this book.

PREFACE

This book started as a challenge from a publishing company to write poetry in December of 2022. Luckily, when I read the rules, they said that I could include previous work. I was thrilled by that concession. That means these poems span a couple decades of my life, though I did take the challenge seriously and get to writing new work. Without further ado, I give you my little book, In Pensive Musing.

Stirring Demons

My sorry, sordid past slips on
Like a velvet glove
Fetch me a fishnet tourniquet
Blades of twisted love

Learning the difference between dirty and filthy
Gently tossed around
Take your lead and meet your eyes
Do it on the ground

Appealing in that it should be unappealing
Contraband in spades
Cuff you to the things you said
Cover me in suedes

Of thinking you are innocent
I've long been disillusioned
But let me think I'm in control
I cling to that delusion

With a dark and twisted Lullaby
You sing me off to sleep

When years melt away like ice
I find myself in deep

What made me reach so readily
For memories far within?
Why did you help me awaken
A past so marred by sin?

Beauty

Beauty like a star
Looking down to catch my eye
Brilliant, cold, and far
Yet burning when drawn near

This beauty condecends to smile
Knowing I can't touch it
Slowing down to speak a while
Full of grace and fear

Yearning strains all sanity
To take this beauty's hand
Commune with all intensity
Peel back the veneer

I seek not lust's dark desire
Nor passion's deep embrace
My soul seeks pure and needful fire
Where reaching minds adhere

I would call this beauty Brother
Dearling, Comrade, Friend
But will one star spark another?
Will the beauty want me here?

Gently Guarded

Gently guard
My war-torn heart
Safe from arrows
Placed apart

The battle's lost
Warzone of love
Silken-voiced angels
Gods above

Fragile embrace
To hide my soul
From the cannon-blast
That won't leave me whole

This sapphire bullet
The gun gone that fired
Becomes a creation
Life being wired

Child of mercy
Child of light
But what did it leave me?
What is this plight?

Through Dangers Untold

A paper-thin veil
Full of monsters and light
The masquerade of eternity
A self-deceptive second sight

Grasping ebony straws
A comforting darkness I know
Violate with awesome energies
Asleep in the afterglow

Welcoming fiendish friends
Temptation's heralds, all
The wile that won my love
A dangerous way to fall.

Stand Up

Your guilt is obscene
Like a glaring litany
That inspires nothing,
Drowning your perceptions
In sorrow and self-pity
Bordering on islands of grief,
Why feel regret for anything
When they feel none
In their baseless retribution
Over wasted moments
That in the end
Weren't really wasted at all?
It's time you stood up
Battling legions of nonsense
Though you may be outnumbered
Possibly outweaponed,
A bit of rebellion
In the name of logic
Can do good for many,
Yet logic is often met
With blindness based in fear
Of approaching nonconformity
And stubbornness based in hatred
Which also stems from fear,
Will they begin to see

You don't necessarily
Have to be the same as all else?
That your flaws and shortfalls
Sometimes can't be helped
And should thus go unpunished?
You struggle as a human
Feeling and reacting,
What do they really expect
When titans of despair
And furies of frustration
Have strong-armed you
And pushed you to the ground?
Fight them now
Unless you'd rather rest in pieces,
Call of the sirens answered
Call of society's all-important "norms,"
Can you find the buried self
That knows better reason
And is not afraid to share it?
Stand alone if you must
But stand up you should.

A Simple Magic

I love the feel of the wind
Tousling my hair as I ponder
And follow my feet
To the places I go,
It makes me feel a little magical
Awakening hidden elvenpaths
As I sing with the songs in my head,
I could descend once again
From the ever-dreaming clouds
But why would you wish that on me?
I feel like an enchantress
A mystic elemental
A magi of the faery sort,
How long will this moment last?
The nearly forgotten realm of fancy
Unfolds its sleeping depths
In a random burst of happy chaos
For once not hinged to nightmare
But instead a sense of quiet strength,
Surrounded in a peaceful power
A splendid thing, this feeling
Rare in its simplicity
May I forever answer its call.

The Moment of Eternity

Morpheus flows in timeless fluidity
Unending vision preserved forever
In the moment of eternity,
The pulse of longing
Creating trysts in twilight realms
Pressing the core of dreaming hearts
In a dance of infinite questing,
Deepness crawls from the nothing of creation
Turning void into presence,
Clasp the weaving loom
Inevitable for all persistence
Only willfulness passes,
Wild roses reach in pricking candor
Whilst the tame burn out in ash.

Dark Side

Give me castles
Give me a knife
Give me wizards
Give me a life

I want your faeries
I want your womb
I want your elves
I want your tomb

I'll take your dreams
I'll take your smile
I'll take your desires
I'll take your guile

I'm your darkest wish
Your deepest fear
I'm your lonely nights
And your every tear

I'm the ghost on your eyelids
The hurt that you sow
The beast in your closet
The worst things you know

I’m that cold nameless dread
You feel when you sleep
The deep senseless longing
In the vigils you keep

I’m the guilt in your memory
Though you did no wrong
Insecurity’s blanket
Depression’s theme song

I’m the world falling down
As old heartaches renew
I’m that venomous voice
The dark side of you.

Drown

White wind withers the soul
Dredging up memory long since buried at sea
Pandora's box uncovered anew
Pricking the fingers of wandering fate
As water-walls of terror threaten to crash

Swirling soft in a mist of fear
Waiting to smother in waves of knowing
Is ignorance bliss?
Deceptive calm in cool, wet sand
Blind to each grain, emerged in seas of blood

Merely mortal, standing aghast
Waters of the world flooding, rising up
We've learnt nothing new
The same evil engulfs, entrenches, surrounds
Finally, ignorance brings it all down

In folly, we gasp, we drown.

Skeletons

Moth-eaten skeletons in the closet
Brush them off
Teach them how to dance
Fill in the holes
Oil the joints
Turn the stage lights on
Show the world your skeletons
What really could go wrong?

My Muse

The muse dips his quill again
Into my inkwell, my blood
Gives it to my waiting hands
He commands and I obey,
I must write once again.

His whisper tortures my ears
The wound held wide open,
"We've awaited your return
And we will not be kept silent,"
Echoes his dark refrain

Vibrant chaos, worlds within
Crying out to be released
A hundred voices screaming
Vying for their words to be spoken
Yet what have I to gain?

I would shut them out today
But no, he gives me parchment,
His voice fills my mind and soul
"Give us life once more, child
Your dreams are our domain."

Battle wages, written or not

Their dream and my nightmare,
Irreparably twined in painful bliss
As they surround me completely
Falling like blood-red rain.

Carry me back to reality
He drives me to the world
And the world drives me back,
The Mists surround, grey and lonely
For my muse is often pain.

Freedom

Mysterious freedom
Draped in a sense of timid inspiration
It twists and curls
Mingling with trepidated longing
Twining with lunatic notions
Of remaining lost in dream
But reality calls now
Trumpeting a reveille of irresistible truths
Waking us all
With an enigmatic blast of mixed emotions,
Don't need to float today
We drift away under the clouds
Storm grey, perfect white, deepest sky-bright blue
Elevated in a breathless wind of beauty,
Things to do, to feel, to be
A musical sea of changes
Freedom tastes of reality.

Him

Beautiful like a Picasso
You don't see it at first
But it's there.
Deep, like an entire spectrum
Each pigment staining my conscience
Telling me something true,
His soul is like agrimony
A balm for the malignant
Dying my heart a sunshine hue,
He wraps me in sackcloth of adoration
Submission to a pious art
Bound in perpetuity.

Twilight

Darkening clouds lined with pink feathered flame
And a gibbous moon come too soon from whence it came
The pale sky grows darker as the sun says its goodbyes
And plants prepare to dew up with the tears that each one cries
Darkness creatures begin to wake from fitful rest
While each creature of the light retires to its nest
This meeting between dark and light
This convergence between day and night
Holds the restless, unsure magic of twilight.

Funny Farm

Welcome to the funny farm, where everything's
a mess
Cows walk on rooftops and the rooster wears a
dress
The pigs wear pink tutus as they attempt to
dance
And chickens chase the well-dressed horse to try
to find romance
A donkey makes himself out to be an ass
Trying to chase down and seduce a pretty lass
But the farmer's daughter won't have that's of
course
Cuz she's already dating that sought-after,
well-dressed horse
She's hated by the chickens for that very fact
Though she doesn't know that cuz she's not
well-known for tact
Surprisingly enough, the farmer sure is lazy
I advise you to stay away from this farm so
crazy
But if you go anyway, whatever will be will be
But if you go there, keep away from me.

The Sum of All Men

The soul of a poet
The voice of an angel
The face of a Botticelli
The heart of a prince
A philosopher's mind
A muscular demi-god's body
Chivalrous values
Noble intent
The charm of a handsome gypsy
The fairest complexion
Mysterious eyes
Does such a man exist for me?

Faith

Faith can build a tower
Faith can make it fall
Faith can have the power
To shake the souls of all
Faith can move a mountain
Faith can keep it still
Faith is like a fountain
That feeds the strength of will
Faith can nurture love
Faith can temper hate
Faith in God above
Can help you shape your fate.

Momento Morte

A murdering monster filled with light
A deadly soft embrace
Hell's bells ringing bright
Gentleman death in silk and lace
Come to put the candles out
Invoke eternal repose
A final silent shout
The canker in the heart of the rose
The reaper at his duty
His lovely, frightening call
In death, such morbid beauty
The dooming specter finds us all.

As I Was Taken

(I feel I should warn those of a sensitive bent that I wrote this poem while I was suffering an episode of sexual assault-related PTSD.)

Loathsome to be touched in hate
The devil's tongue wrapped round my throat
Choking out life I never knew was there
Draining dry the veins of my soul

Sucked into undercurrents of fear
Dripping founts of blood and worse
Violation of mind and body
Twisted in a screaming, silent nightmare

Take this sickening pain from me
Clean the filth that permeates my flesh
Remove me from this hateful place
I'll hide in the shadow of your darkness.

Married Love

I clasp both the hands
That've loved every part of me
Bask in the moment
Kiss his knuckles gently

Repeat the three words
That mean more than parlance
A radiance fills us
In our comfortable romance

Two genuine smiles glimmer
Prodigious, cheesy, but authentic
Happiness in unity
Springing forth concentric

I flood with deep warmth
Near my great teller of tales
Wrapped in his fancy
All my anxiety pales,

I recall virtue and oaths
A mirror that echoes infinity
My love across from me
Kneeling 'fore divinity

Hands clasped in holy emblem
Troth to God and each other
Desire in a sacred space
Eternity with another.

Twinkling Tomorrow

Yesterday's twinkling tomorrow loomed
Ethereal prayers passed into the night
Where daybreak saw not my tears
Could this memory linger on?
Where mystery echoes with surreal breath
Penetrated by perfected desire
Painted thoughts of the heart
Where the place I long for lies.

www.ingramcontent.com/pod-product-compliance
Lightning Source LLC
Chambersburg PA
CBHW051752130826
49812CB00033B/1111
* 9 7 8 9 3 5 7 2 1 2 3 6 6 *